TEEDIE

★ ★ ★ ★ ★ ★ ★ ★ ★ ★ ★ ★ ★ ★ ★ ★ ★

The Story of Young Teddy Roosevelt

In loving memory of my brother, Ty

Houghton Mifflin Books for Children is an imprint of
Houghton Mifflin Harcourt Publishing Company.
www.hmhbooks.com

The text of this book is set in Hightower.
The illustrations are pen and ink and watercolor on paper, as well as digitally created.
Book design by Carol Goldenberg

Library of Congress Cataloging-in-Publication Data
Brown, Don, 1949–
Teedie : the story of young Teddy Roosevelt /
written and illustrated by Don Brown.
p. cm.
Includes bibliographical references and index.
ISBN 978-0-618-17999-2 (alk. paper)
1. Roosevelt, Theodore, 1858–1919—Childhood and youth—Juvenile literature.
2. Presidents—United States—Biography—Juvenile literature. I. Title.
E757.B876 2009
973.91′1092—dc22
[B]
2008033879

Printed in China
CAC 10 9 8 7 6 5 4 3 2 1

TEEDIE

★ ★

The Story of Young Teddy Roosevelt

by Don Brown

HOUGHTON MIFFLIN BOOKS FOR CHILDREN

HOUGHTON MIFFLIN HARCOURT

BOSTON 2009

TEN-YEAR-OLD TEEDIE played with his sisters and brother in their fine house on Twenty-eighth Street. He liked being there, for Teedie was a timid homebody who studied with visiting tutors instead of going to school. Small for his age, he had weak eyes and frail muscles. Sickly lungs left him gasping. He'd later describe himself as "delicate." Surely, a boy like him would expect nothing more than the most unremarkable of lives. But Teedie—Teddy Roosevelt—had different thoughts of what his future would be.

The Roosevelts were one of New York City's wealthiest families, and Teedie enjoyed uncommon privileges such as servants, grand vacations to foreign lands, and summer houses.

Teedie, his brother, Ellie, and his sisters, Bamie and Conie, loved summers in the country. They had cats, dogs, rabbits, and a Shetland pony named General Grant. Their father taught them to climb trees. They ran barefoot, picked apples, gathered nuts, and hunted frogs successfully and woodchucks unsuccessfully. They built wigwams in the woods.

But the Roosevelts' wealth couldn't protect Teedie from asthma. The disease made him struggle for air, and gave him the terrifying feeling of slowly drowning. Asthma puzzled doctors, and there were no clear remedies. Frightened and unsure what to do, his father paced the room with little Teedie in his arms or his mother rubbed his chest with her gentle fingers. They took Teedie on long carriage drives in search of a helpful "change of air." Panicked, they even experimented with wild cures, sometimes having young Teedie gulp coffee or puff on a cigar. Asthma would always trouble him, deviling him into adulthood from time to time.

Despite his weak body, Teedie had a strong mind.
He loved reading.
"My father and mother [had] the good sense not to try to get me to
read anything I did not like," he said, adding, "I do not believe a child's
book is really good unless grown-ups get something out of it."

He had boundless curiosity. Once he walked down the street and spotted a dead seal laid out on a slab of wood.

"That seal filled me with every possible feeling of romance and adventure," he said. "I carefully made a record of utterly useless measurements and at once began to write a natural history of my own on the strength of that seal. I did get the seal's skull, and promptly started the Roosevelt Museum of Natural History."

It was a natural turn for a boy's whose father had helped found the American Museum of Natural History in New York City.

In 1872, Papa Roosevelt gave his thirteen-year-old son a shotgun. While hunting, Teedie noticed his companions saw things to shoot that he could not see at all. And they could read distant billboards, while he was unable to even see the letters. Neither he nor his family had ever noticed his nearsightedness before.

He was fitted for eyeglasses, and an entirely new world opened for him.

"I had no idea how beautiful the world was," he remarked.

Still, Teedie's frail body troubled his father. "You have the mind but you have not the body, and without the help of the body the mind cannot go as far as it should," he told Teedie. "You must make your body. It is hard drudgery to make one's body, but I know you will do it."

Teedie agreed at once.

He spent hours in the gym, hauling himself up and down horizontal bars

and lifting dumbbells and weights.

He paddled "in the hottest sun, over the roughest water, in the smallest boat."

He rode horses.

On one outing, the horse turned a somersault over a fence.

"After the fall I found I could not use my left arm, so we pounded along. I did not appreciate that my arm was broken for three or four fences," he said.

Yet for all the hard work, Teedie remained undersize, nervous, and timid.

Enduring another asthma attack, he was sent away to the mountains to recover. While traveling alone by stagecoach to meet friends, he chanced upon two bullies.

"They proceeded to make life miserable for me. I made up my mind that I would not again be put in such a helpless position. I started to learn to box," he later remembered.

He was a slow and awkward pupil. But he entered a match and, to everyone's surprise, won.

"This was one of my exceedingly rare athletic triumphs," he said. The pewter mug he was rewarded became one his most prized possessions.

By 1876, Teedie was known to many as Teddy. He enrolled in Cambridge's famous Harvard University.

"I thoroughly enjoyed Harvard, and I am sure it did me good, but only in the general effect, for there was very little in my actual studies which helped me in after life," he admitted.

After graduation, he wanted not to "rise on any else's shoulders": "[I] hoped only to be given chances that my deeds and abilities warranted. I did not wish what I did not earn."

He considered a science career. He wrote a book about the War of 1812, the first of many books he'd write. He studied the law, a bit. He entered politics and was elected to the New York Assembly.

He married and had a daughter. But tragedy struck and his wife died. Hoping to mend his broken heart, he fled to the Dakota Badlands, leaving his baby in his sister's care.

Teddy wasn't a great cowboy
but an enthusiastic one.

He lassoed calves.

Rode on roundups.

Headed off stampedes.

Broke broncos.

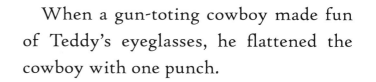

When a gun-toting cowboy made fun of Teddy's eyeglasses, he flattened the cowboy with one punch.

It was a powerful, broad-shouldered Teddy who returned to New York in 1886.

He remarried and fathered five more children.

In 1895 he was appointed New York City police commissioner and put down lawlessness and disorder. His good work attracted the president of the United States, who made him assistant secretary of the navy.

When war started between America and Spain in 1898, he formed a volunteer cavalry called the Rough Riders. At San Juan, Puerto Rico, Colonel Teddy Roosevelt led his men in a charge against enemy trenches. People called him gallant and courageous and recommended him for the Medal of Honor.

Famous now, he was elected governor of New York, and then vice president of the United States. In 1901, Teddy Roosevelt became president of the United States, the youngest ever at forty-two.

Assassinated 1901

1900

President Wm McKinley

Vice President Teddy Roosevelt

Teddy decided, "[America] will not be a good place for any of us to live in if it is not a reasonably good place for all of us to live in."

Taking his own advice of "Seize the moment" and "Do what you can, with what you have, where you are," Teddy . . .

Policed big businesses and demanded they act fairly.

Protected the Grand Canyon and other wild places.

Built a canal in Panama.

Ended a war between the Russians and Japanese and won the Nobel Peace Prize.

President of the
United States
1901

Fights Business Trusts
Establishes National
Parks & Preserves
Builds Panama Canal
Ends Russian-Japanese War,
Wins Nobel Peace Prize·1905
Dies January 6, 1919

His success was "Remarkable!" "Amazing!" "Extraordinary!"
Yet Teddy claimed he was just average.
But the world knew differently: The undersize boy had
become a larger-than-life man.

Author's Note

THE ROOSEVELTS' WEALTH AND STATUS inoculated them from the routine hardships and difficulties experienced by most others; Theodore's father escaped military service during the Civil War by hiring a substitute to serve for him. Still, the family embraced community service, and the senior Roosevelt assisted soldiers during the war, helped the poor, and later was a driving force behind the establishment of the American Museum of Natural History.

Young Theodore's curiosity and tenacity carried him through Harvard and the launch of his political career. He entered the New York Assembly, and his reputation grew.

On February 14, 1884, both Teddy's mother and wife died unexpectedly. In his diary that day, he scrawled a large X followed by "The light has gone out of my life."

He fled to the Dakota Badlands and found healing there. He returned to New York, remarried, and restarted his political career. His good work and courage attracted attention, and he won important government positions. He soon found himself with the vice presidency, and then, at the assassination of McKinley, the presidency. A second term followed.

In 1912 he made a bid for a third presidential term—not with the Republican Party endorsement, but with his own Bull Moose Party. During the campaign, a would-be assassin shot Teddy in the chest. Teddy delivered a ninety-minute speech before seeking medical attention. He eventually came in second in the three-person presidential election.

Two years later, Teddy traveled to Brazil with an expedition for the American Museum of Natural History. It was a difficult journey and nearly killed him.

During the First World War, Teddy offered to raise and lead a volunteer division in France. President Wilson refused. Teddy's son Quentin joined the air corps and was killed.

In 1933, Teddy's distant cousin Franklin Delano Roosevelt became president. FDR was married to Teddy's niece, Eleanor.

In 1919, sixty-year-old Teddy Roosevelt died in his sleep in his Long Island home, Sagamore Hill.

★ ★ ★

Bibliography

McCullough, David G. *Mornings on Horseback*. New York: Simon and Schuster, 1981.

Robinson, Corinne Roosevelt. *My Brother, Theodore Roosevelt*. New York: Scribner's Sons, 1921.

Roosevelt, Theodore. *Diaries of Boyhood and Youth*. New York: Charles Scribner's Sons, 1928.

———. *Theodore Roosevelt: An Autobiography*. New York: Macmillan, 1913.

www.theodoreroosevelt.org/life/timeline.htm